God's Heart for Women Study Manual

Empowering Women to Answer Their Call in Life and Ministry

Rhonda Garver

Copyright 2024–Harrison House

All rights reserved. This book is protected by the copyright laws of the United States of America. This book may not be copied or reprinted for commercial gain or profit. The use of short quotations or occasional page copying for personal or group study is permitted and encouraged. Permission will be granted upon request. Unless otherwise indicated, all scripture quotations are taken from the *King James Version* of the Bible. Used by permission. All rights reserved.

All emphasis within Scripture quotations is the author's own. Please note that Harrison House's publishing style capitalizes certain pronouns in Scripture that refer to the Father, Son, and Holy Spirit, and may differ from some publishers' styles. Take note that the name satan and related names are not capitalized. We choose not to acknowledge him, even to the point of violating grammatical rules.

Harrison House P.O. Box 310, Shippensburg, PA 17257-0310

This book and all other Harrison House's books are available at Christian bookstores and distributors worldwide.

Reach us on the Internet: www.harrisonhouse.com.

ISBN 13 TP: 9781667510620

ISBN 13 eBook: 9781667510637

Contents

1. The Journey Begins — 1
2. In the Beginning — 9
3. But What About...? — 15
4. After the Fall — 23
5. Jesus' Heart Toward Women — 29
6. Prophecies Regarding Last-Days Women — 37
7. Paul and Women — 45
8. Who May Minister? — 51
9. "Let the Woman Learn in Silence" — 57
10. "It Is Not Permitted unto Them to Speak" — 63
11. How Did We Get Here? — 69
12. Free to Answer His Call — 75

About the Author — 81
About the Publisher — 83

Chapter 1

The Journey Begins

"Study to shew thyself approved unto God, a workman that needeth not to be ashamed, rightly dividing the word of truth." (2 Timothy 2:15, KJV)

She sat across the desk from me, her shoulders heaving from quiet sobs, her tears streaming through her fingers, which were tightly clasped to her face. "I don't know what to do," she began. "I know with all my heart that God called me to the ministry, but does the Bible really say I can't obey Him?" The pain in her voice was unmistakable. She had just come from an encounter that had left her shaken. Some local pastors had confronted her about accepting invitations to minister, accusing her of stepping outside the bounds of God's order. The weight of their words, especially the insinuation that her beloved grandfather would have been ashamed of her actions, had pierced her heart deeply.

This moment marked the beginning of my deep journey into the Word of God concerning women in ministry. Though I had been in pastoral ministry for over two decades, I had never extensively studied this topic for myself. I had a general belief that God called and anointed both men and women, but the tears of this young woman, combined with my own invitation to teach on the subject, propelled me into deeper study. I needed answers, not just for her, but for every woman struggling with the same questions.

As I searched the scriptures, one truth became clear: God's Word must be the foundation of our beliefs. We cannot shape doctrine based on opinions, tradition, or personal preference. If God truly called women, then His Word would confirm it. If He did not, then we needed to align with that as well. The Word alone had to be our guide.

This chapter is not merely about theology; it is about truth that sets people free. It is about obedience to God and the courage to step into His calling, regardless of opposition. As we begin this journey together, I challenge you: have you ever deeply studied this issue for yourself? What formed your beliefs? And most importantly—are you willing to lay aside every preconceived notion and allow God's Word to speak for itself?

Focus Point

"Now the Berean Jews were of more noble character than those in Thessalonica, for they received the message with great eagerness and examined the Scriptures every day to see if what Paul said was true." (Acts 17:11, NIV)

This verse highlights the necessity of diligent study. The Bereans were commended for verifying the truth of what they were taught. In the same way, we must approach Scripture with an open heart, willing to let God's Word, not human tradition, define our beliefs about women in ministry.

Main Theme

The heart of this chapter is the necessity of seeking God's truth in Scripture, rather than relying on traditions or opinions. Many sincere believers are passionate about what they think the Bible says about women in ministry, yet few have done a thorough study. Just as God has used both men and women throughout history, He continues to do so today. The question is not whether culture accepts it, but whether Scripture affirms it.

"The truth is not shaped by tradition; it is revealed in God's unchanging Word."

Key Scriptures

- *"Study to shew thyself approved unto God, a workman that needeth not to be ashamed, rightly dividing the word of truth."* (2 Timothy 2:15, KJV)
- *"There is neither Jew nor Greek, slave nor free, male nor female, for you are all one in Christ Jesus."* (Galatians 3:28, NKJV)

- *"God is not a man, that He should lie, nor a son of man, that He should change His mind."* (Numbers 23:19, NKJV)

Key Points

- **God Calls Both Men and Women** The Bible is filled with examples of women whom God called to leadership and ministry, including Deborah, Miriam, and Huldah. His call is not limited by gender.
- **The Word, Not Tradition, Determines Truth** Many beliefs about women in ministry stem from traditions rather than deep biblical study. We must seek what Scripture actually says.
- **God's Anointing Confirms His Call** If God did not approve of women ministering, why has He anointed so many throughout history to preach, prophesy, and lead?
- **Authority Comes From God, Not Culture** Throughout Scripture, God has called and empowered individuals regardless of societal norms. His Kingdom operates by His order, not human hierarchy.
- **The Berean Model: Search the Scriptures** We must follow the example of the Bereans and study deeply for ourselves, rather than relying on secondhand theology.
- **Women Have Historically Advanced the Gospel** From the early church to modern revivals, women have been instrumental in carrying the message of Christ. This alone challenges restrictive views.
- **Obedience to God Trumps Human Opinion** If God calls a woman to preach, who are we to oppose Him? Our responsibility is to obey Him, not to fear human disapproval.

Journaling Questions

Journaling provides a means to process what God is revealing. As you engage with this chapter, take time to reflect on your beliefs about women in ministry. Have they been shaped by personal study or by others' opinions? Through journaling, you can clarify areas where God is speaking to you and identify where further study is needed. Self-reflection is essential for spiritual growth, allowing us to embrace biblical truth over cultural norms.

As you answer the following questions, consider how they challenge or affirm your understanding of God's heart for women in ministry.

Examining Your Beliefs

What are your current beliefs about women in ministry, and where did they originate?

_____

The Influence of Tradition

Have your views on this topic been shaped more by church tradition or by personal Bible study?

_____

Scriptural Evidence

What scriptures have you personally studied that affirm or challenge your perspective?

_____

God's Call

Have you ever felt a calling to serve in ministry? If so, how have you responded?

_____
_____
_____
_____
_____
_____

Aligning With Truth

What steps can you take to ensure that your beliefs align fully with God's Word rather than human opinion?

_____
_____
_____
_____
_____
_____

Actionable Steps

Cultivate a Heart for Truth
Commit to searching the Scriptures on this topic with an open heart, asking God to reveal His truth.

Equip Yourself With Knowledge
Study the biblical accounts of women in ministry and take note of God's calling and anointing on their lives.

Engage in Courageous Conversations
Discuss this topic with other believers, sharing what you are learning and encouraging others to study it for themselves.

Personal Reflection

God's Word is alive, and it speaks clearly when we are willing to listen. As we examine our beliefs, we must be willing to surrender any preconceived notions that do not align with Scripture. Have you been willing to truly search the Word for yourself, or have you relied on secondhand theology?

The journey toward truth requires humility and a willingness to grow. Studying this issue deeply may challenge what you have always believed, but it will also strengthen your confidence in God's calling for both men and women. Will you allow the Word of God to shape your understanding?

What will you do with the truth you uncover? Will you embrace it, or will you hold on to tradition? How will you respond to God's call?

Closing Prayer: *Lord, thank You for Your Word, which is a lamp to my feet and a light to my path. Help me to seek Your truth with an open heart, unhindered by tradition or fear. Give me wisdom to discern Your call and courage to walk in obedience. May my life reflect Your will, and may I always stand firm in the truth of Your Word. In Jesus' name, Amen.*

Chapter 2

In the Beginning

"So God created man in His own image; in the image of God He created him; male and female He created them." (Genesis 1:27, NKJV)

The young woman sat across from me, her Bible open, her face a mix of frustration and longing. "I was told that God made women second because we were meant to be under men's leadership. Is that really true?" she asked. Her question was not one of mere curiosity—it was one of identity. She wanted to know if, from the very beginning, God had ordained women to be lesser than men. For years, she had accepted what had been taught, but something inside her urged her to dig deeper, to see if what she had always believed aligned with Scripture.

I understood her struggle. Many people have been taught that the creation order in Genesis establishes male dominance and female subordination. But is that really what Scripture teaches? Does God's original design place men in authority over women, or is there something more profound hidden in the beauty of creation?

As I studied the opening chapters of Genesis, I began to see a breathtaking truth emerge. Man and woman were created together in God's image—both bearing His likeness, both carrying His divine purpose. There was no hint of hierarchy, no indication that one was superior to the other. Instead, they were called to rule together, reflecting the perfect unity found within the Trinity itself.

If we are to understand God's heart for women, we must go back to the beginning. We must strip away the cultural interpretations that have clouded our vision and see what God truly intended when He fashioned male and female in His image. The question is, are we willing to see what Scripture actually says, even if it challenges our long-held assumptions?

Focus Point

"Then the Lord God said, 'It is not good that man should be alone; I will make him a helper comparable to him.'" (Genesis 2:18, NKJV)

This verse is often misunderstood as implying inferiority. However, the Hebrew word for *helper* (*ezer*) is used elsewhere in Scripture to describe God Himself as a helper to Israel. It does not imply subordination, but rather strength and partnership. Woman was created as an equal counterpart, not as a lesser being.

Main Theme

The foundation of God's design for men and women is equality and partnership. Both were made in His image, given dominion, and called to steward creation together. Any doctrine that diminishes the role of women in God's plan contradicts the original intent seen in Genesis. Sin distorted this equality, but through Christ, restoration is possible.

"God's original design was not hierarchy, but harmony."

Key Scriptures

- *"So God created man in His own image; in the image of God He created him; male and female He created them."* (Genesis 1:27, NKJV)
- *"Then God blessed them, and God said to them, 'Be fruitful and multiply; fill the earth and subdue it; have dominion over the fish of the sea, over the birds of the air, and over every living thing that moves on the earth.'"* (Genesis 1:28, NKJV)
- *"There is neither Jew nor Greek, there is neither slave nor free, there is neither male nor female; for you are all one in Christ Jesus."* (Galatians 3:28, NKJV)

Key Points

- **Created in the Image of God** Both man and woman were made in the image of God, reflecting His nature, authority, and creativity.
- **Equal Dominion and Authority** Genesis 1:28 gives both male and female the command to rule over creation, signifying shared authority.
- **The Meaning of 'Helper'** The word *ezer* used for woman is also used for God, signifying strength and partnership rather than inferiority.
- **The Original Plan Was Partnership** Before the fall, Adam and Eve lived in unity, neither ruling over the other but fulfilling their divine purpose together.
- **Sin Introduced Distortion** The fall introduced division, but Jesus came to restore what was broken, including the unity between men and women.
- **Christ Restores Equality** Through the work of Jesus, believers are restored to their original calling—working together without division.
- **God's Design Stands Above Culture** Many interpretations of gender roles come from culture rather than Scripture. God's design must be our foundation.

Journaling Questions

Journaling allows us to explore the truth of God's Word and compare it to what we have been taught. Take time to reflect on whether your beliefs about gender roles align with the biblical account of creation. Scripture calls us to renew our minds—this is an opportunity to let God's truth shape your understanding.

Through reflection, you may uncover areas where tradition has influenced your perspective more than Scripture. Allow God to guide you in embracing His design for men and women.

Understanding God's Image

How does knowing that both men and women bear God's image change your view of gender roles?

_____
_____
_____
_____

The Power of Partnership

What does the concept of shared dominion in Genesis 1:28 mean for relationships between men and women?

_____
_____
_____
_____
_____
_____

Breaking Cultural Barriers

Are there ways in which cultural traditions have shaped your view of women in the church and society?

_____
_____
_____
_____
_____
_____

Restoration Through Christ

How does Jesus' work on the cross restore God's original intent for men and women?

_____
_____
_____
_____
_____
_____

Aligning With Truth

What steps can you take to ensure your beliefs about gender align with God's Word rather than human tradition?

_____
_____
_____
_____
_____
_____

Actionable Steps

Cultivate Biblical Understanding
Commit to studying the creation narrative in Genesis with fresh eyes, asking God for revelation on His design.

Equip Yourself With Truth
Compare different interpretations of gender roles and evaluate them against Scripture, ensuring that your understanding is rooted in God's Word.

Engage in Meaningful Conversations
Discuss what you are learning with others, challenging assumptions and encouraging biblical truth in your community.

Personal Reflection

Understanding God's heart for men and women begins with recognizing His original design. If we allow tradition or culture to dictate our beliefs, we risk missing the fullness of what God intended. Are you willing to reexamine long-held beliefs in light of Scripture?

The truth of God's Word has the power to dismantle distortions and bring clarity. If we are to walk in the freedom Christ offers, we must be willing to challenge interpretations that contradict His intent. Will you seek God's truth with an open heart?

Closing Prayer: *Lord, thank You for creating both men and women in Your image. Help me to see Your design clearly and to align my heart with Your truth. Remove any misunderstandings I have inherited from tradition, and lead me into a deeper revelation of Your purpose for both men and women. May I walk in the fullness of Your calling, unhindered by human limitations. In Jesus' name, Amen.*

Chapter 3

But What About...?

"All Scripture is given by inspiration of God, and is profitable for doctrine, for reproof, for correction, for instruction in righteousness." (2 Timothy 3:16, NKJV)

She hesitated before asking the question that had been on her heart for years. "I hear what you're saying about God calling women, but what about Paul's words? Doesn't he say women should be silent? And that they shouldn't have authority over men?" Her voice carried the weight of someone torn between personal conviction and scriptural interpretation. She wanted to believe that God had called her, but these verses loomed over her like an insurmountable barrier.

Her struggle is not uncommon. Many who embrace the idea of God calling both men and women to ministry still wrestle with passages that appear to restrict women's roles. These verses have been quoted for centuries to silence women, limiting their influence in the church. But is that what Scripture truly teaches? Do these verses provide a universal restriction, or is there a deeper context that reveals God's heart?

As I studied these difficult passages, I discovered that Scripture must be interpreted as a whole. We cannot isolate a few verses while ignoring the broader biblical narrative of God using women in powerful ways. The Bible never contradicts itself—if God anointed women like Deborah, Priscilla, and Junia, then Paul's words must be understood in light of their historical and cultural setting.

This chapter invites you to step beyond surface-level readings and dig deeper into God's Word. If we believe that "all Scripture is inspired by God," then we must approach these texts with both reverence and a commitment to understanding them fully. Are you willing to seek the truth, even if it challenges traditional interpretations?

Focus Point

"There is neither Jew nor Greek, there is neither slave nor free, there is neither male nor female; for you are all one in Christ Jesus." (Galatians 3:28, NKJV)

This verse speaks to the heart of the gospel—unity in Christ. If the New Testament proclaims equality in salvation and spiritual inheritance, then any interpretation of Paul's writings that implies permanent subordination of women must be examined carefully.

Main Theme

Difficult passages about women in ministry must be understood in the full context of Scripture. Paul's writings were addressing specific cultural issues in certain churches, not establishing universal prohibitions. Throughout the Bible, God calls and anoints women, demonstrating His intention for them to serve alongside men in advancing His Kingdom.

"Scripture interprets Scripture—one passage cannot negate the entire narrative of God's redemptive plan."

Key Scriptures

- *"Let a woman learn in silence with all submission. And I do not permit a woman to teach or to have authority over a man, but to be in silence."* (1 Timothy 2:11-12, NKJV)
- *"Greet Andronicus and Junia, my countrymen and my fellow prisoners, who are of note among the apostles, who also were in Christ before me."* (Romans 16:7, NKJV)
- *"Priscilla and Aquila took him aside and explained to him the way of God more accurately."* (Acts 18:26, NKJV)

Key Points

- **Context Matters in Interpretation** Paul's letters addressed specific cultural and church issues; they were not blanket restrictions meant for all time.
- **Women Were Leaders in the Early Church** Paul himself recognized and affirmed women like Phoebe, Junia, and Priscilla, showing that women did teach and lead.
- **Silence Does Not Mean Inactivity** When Paul instructed women to be silent in church, he was addressing a disorderly issue in Corinth, not making a universal law.
- **Authority and Teaching Roles** The Greek word for "authority" in 1 Timothy 2:12 (*authentein*) is rarely used in Scripture and carries connotations of domination rather than biblical leadership.
- **Paul's Consistency in Supporting Women** If Paul truly meant to forbid women from teaching, why did he commend them for doing so in other passages?
- **The Gospel Restores Equality** Just as Christ removed barriers between Jew and Gentile, He also removed the distinctions that limited women's spiritual roles.
- **God Calls Whom He Chooses** If God has placed His anointing on a woman, human interpretations cannot stand against His divine calling.

Journaling Questions

Many have accepted restrictive interpretations without deeply studying these passages for themselves. Journaling provides a space to examine your beliefs in light of Scripture. Consider whether your views on women in ministry have been shaped by cultural assumptions or by personal study of God's Word.

Reflection allows for transformation. As you explore these questions, let the Holy Spirit guide you into deeper truth, removing any barriers that prevent you from embracing God's full design for men and women.

Understanding Paul's Words

How have you previously understood Paul's instructions about women in ministry? Have you studied them in depth?

The Role of Women in the Early Church

What do passages about Priscilla, Junia, and Phoebe reveal about women's leadership in the early church?

Examining Cultural Context

How does knowing the cultural background of Paul's letters change your understanding of his words?

The Fullness of God's Calling

If you are a woman, do you feel fully free to pursue God's calling? If you are a man, do you affirm and support the women God has called?

_____
_____
_____
_____
_____
_____

Aligning With Truth

What steps can you take to ensure your understanding of this issue is based on Scripture rather than tradition?

_____
_____
_____
_____
_____

Actionable Steps

Cultivate a Spirit of Inquiry
Commit to studying difficult passages with an open heart, seeking understanding rather than reinforcing assumptions.

Equip Yourself With Biblical Knowledge
Research historical and cultural contexts behind Paul's writings to gain a clearer perspective.

Engage in Constructive Dialogue
Have conversations with others about what you're learning, challenging long-held misconceptions with biblical truth.

Personal Reflection

Interpreting Scripture requires diligence, humility, and a willingness to let go of preconceived ideas. If we hold tightly to tradition at the expense of truth, we risk missing God's design. Are you willing to let Scripture, rather than opinion, shape your understanding of this issue?

Many women have wrestled with these questions, longing to obey God yet feeling restrained by misunderstood texts. But as we examine Scripture fully, we see a pattern of God using both men and women to accomplish His purposes. Will you embrace the fullness of His calling?

If God is revealing new truth to you, how will you respond? Will you seek deeper study, or will you settle for tradition?

Closing Prayer: *Lord, thank You for Your Word, which is living and active. Help me to approach Scripture with an open heart, seeking truth over tradition. Where I have misunderstood, bring clarity. Where I have resisted, bring surrender. Let me see Your design clearly and support Your calling in all Your people. In Jesus' name, Amen.*

Chapter 4

After the Fall

"To the woman He said: 'I will greatly multiply your sorrow and your conception; in pain you shall bring forth children; your desire shall be for your husband, and he shall rule over you.'"
(Genesis 3:16, NKJV)

She sat quietly, staring at the words on the page, struggling to reconcile what she had been taught with what she was now reading for herself. "So, was it always God's plan for men to rule over women? Or was this part of the curse?" she asked. It was a question I had wrestled with myself—one that had been used to justify male dominance for centuries. Yet, the more I studied, the more I realized that Genesis 3:16 was not a divine commandment, but a consequence of sin.

The fall of humanity introduced disorder into God's perfect creation. Where there was once harmony between men and women, there was now conflict. The unity that had characterized Adam and Eve's relationship was fractured by sin, leading to domination and suffering. But was this God's intention? Or was it a tragic distortion of His original design?

If we misunderstand Genesis 3:16, we risk normalizing brokenness instead of seeking restoration. Jesus came to reverse the effects of the fall, yet many still operate under the curse, believing it to be God's will. But if Christ has redeemed us, should we not also expect redemption in our relationships and roles?

This chapter challenges us to look beyond the curse and embrace God's plan for restoration. If the fall brought division, Christ brings unity. If sin led to hierarchy, grace leads to partnership. Are we willing to walk in the fullness of that redemption?

Focus Point

"For as in Adam all die, even so in Christ all shall be made alive." (1 Corinthians 15:22, NKJV)

This verse reminds us that while Adam's sin brought death and disorder, Christ's redemptive work brings restoration. We are not bound by the consequences of the fall—we are invited into the fullness of new life in Him.

Main Theme

The fall distorted God's perfect design for humanity, introducing pain, suffering, and imbalance in relationships. But through Christ, the curse is reversed, and we are called back into the partnership God originally intended. Understanding the difference between consequence and commandment is essential in embracing God's heart for men and women.

"God's redemption restores what sin has broken."

Key Scriptures

- *"To the woman He said: 'I will greatly multiply your sorrow and your conception; in pain you shall bring forth children; your desire shall be for your husband, and he shall rule over you.'"* (Genesis 3:16, NKJV)
- *"Christ has redeemed us from the curse of the law, having become a curse for us."* (Galatians 3:13, NKJV)
- *"There is neither Jew nor Greek, there is neither slave nor free, there is neither male nor female; for you are all one in Christ Jesus."* (Galatians 3:28, NKJV)

Key Points

- **The Fall Introduced Division** Before sin, Adam and Eve operated in unity. After sin, their relationship became strained, marked by struggle and domination.
- **Genesis 3:16 Is Not a Commandment** God did not *command* men to rule over

women; He foretold the consequence of sin. This was a declaration of brokenness, not divine order.

- **Jesus Came to Reverse the Curse** Through His death and resurrection, Jesus restored what was lost in the fall, including the equality and partnership between men and women.
- **Biblical Redemption Includes Relationships** If Christ's redemption applies to sin, sickness, and death, it also applies to the broken relationships caused by the fall.
- **God's Original Design Remains the Goal** God never abandoned His original plan of harmony. The New Testament reaffirms the call for mutual submission and partnership in Christ.
- **Cultural Norms Must Not Define Theology** Many interpretations of gender roles are based on historical traditions rather than biblical truth. We must return to Scripture's full narrative.
- **The Church Must Model Redemption** If we truly believe in Christ's transformative power, we must embrace His work of restoration in every area, including gender relationships.

Journaling Questions

Journaling allows us to process how deeply we've internalized the effects of the fall and whether we have unknowingly accepted the curse as God's will. Take time to reflect on how your understanding of Genesis 3:16 has shaped your views on gender roles and relationships. Have you assumed hierarchy was part of God's plan, or do you recognize it as part of the curse?

Through reflection, we can invite God to renew our thinking and align our hearts with His redemptive work. Ask the Holy Spirit to reveal areas where tradition has shaped your beliefs more than biblical truth.

Understanding the Consequence

How does seeing Genesis 3:16 as a consequence rather than a command change your perspective on gender roles?

_____
_____
_____
_____

Redemption and Relationships

In what ways does Jesus' redemptive work impact the dynamics between men and women today?

_____
_____
_____
_____
_____
_____

Breaking Free from the Curse

Are there areas in your life where you have unknowingly accepted brokenness as God's will instead of seeking His restoration?

_____
_____
_____
_____
_____
_____

Returning to God's Design

What steps can you take to align your understanding of men and women with God's original plan in Genesis 1 and 2?

_____
_____
_____
_____
_____
_____

Living in Redemption

How can you actively participate in restoring biblical partnership and equality in your church and community?

_____
_____
_____
_____
_____

Actionable Steps

Cultivate a Renewed Mind
Commit to studying the full biblical narrative, recognizing where sin distorted God's design and where Christ brings restoration.

Seek His Word Daily
Compare traditional interpretations of Genesis 3:16 with the broader message of redemption in Scripture. Seek biblical resources that affirm God's full plan.

Engage in Community
Actively support and encourage mutual respect, partnership, and biblical equality in your relationships, church, and ministry.

Personal Reflection

Understanding the effects of the fall allows us to see how desperately we need Christ's redemption. If we do not recognize Genesis 3:16 as a consequence of sin, we risk living under a mindset that normalizes brokenness instead of seeking restoration. Are you willing to let go of old assumptions and embrace the fullness of God's redemption?

God's heart has always been for unity, partnership, and restoration. When we accept Christ's work in its entirety, we allow Him to heal not just our personal sins, but the broken relationships that sin has caused. Will you step into the freedom He offers?

If Christ has redeemed us from the curse, why would we continue to live under its effects? How will you choose to walk in His redemption?

_____
_____
_____
_____
_____
_____
_____
_____
_____
_____
_____
_____
_____
_____
_____
_____
_____
_____
_____
_____
_____
_____
_____

Closing Prayer: *Lord, thank You for Your redemptive power that restores all things. Help me to see the difference between what You have commanded and what sin has corrupted. Align my heart with Your truth and free me from any mindset that accepts brokenness as normal. May my life reflect the fullness of Your redemption, and may I walk in the freedom Christ has purchased for me. In Jesus' name, Amen.*

Chapter 5

Jesus' Heart Toward Women

"But Jesus said, 'Let her alone. Why do you trouble her? She has done a good work for Me.'" (Mark 14:6, NKJV)

She stood trembling at the edge of the crowd, clutching a small alabaster jar in her hands. The voices of the men around her were sharp with judgment, condemning her very presence. But Jesus, the one she had risked everything to see, did not push her away. Instead, He received her worship. "Let her alone," He said firmly. "She has done a good work for Me." In a culture where women were often dismissed, Jesus saw her, defended her, and honored her act of devotion.

The radical love of Jesus toward women was evident throughout His ministry. He spoke with them publicly, something unheard of for a Jewish rabbi. He taught them alongside His disciples, healed them, and entrusted them with the most profound truths of His mission. Time and again, Jesus broke societal norms to restore dignity to women, treating them as full participants in God's Kingdom.

Yet, for centuries, the church has wrestled with understanding and applying Jesus' example. While some have followed His model of inclusion, others have reverted to cultural traditions that diminish women's roles. But if Jesus is our perfect example, should we not follow His lead in honoring and empowering women in ministry?

This chapter challenges us to see women through the eyes of Jesus. If He consistently uplifted, taught, and entrusted women with His message, how can we do anything less? Are we willing to align our views with His heart?

Focus Point

"Then He said to her, 'Daughter, your faith has made you well. Go in peace, and be healed of your affliction.'" (Mark 5:34, NKJV)

This verse captures Jesus' deep compassion for women. He not only healed physical ailments but also restored dignity, calling them "Daughter," a term of love and belonging. His words healed more than her body—they affirmed her worth.

Main Theme

Jesus' interactions with women reveal His heart for their dignity, calling, and inclusion in His Kingdom. He did not see them as secondary but as vital to His mission. By examining His encounters with women, we gain a clearer understanding of how He calls us to treat and honor them today.

"Jesus did not merely tolerate women; He empowered them."

Key Scriptures

- *"Let her alone. Why do you trouble her? She has done a good work for Me."* (Mark 14:6, NKJV)
- *"Now it came to pass, afterward, that He went through every city and village, preaching and bringing the glad tidings of the kingdom of God. And the twelve were with Him, and certain women who had been healed of evil spirits and infirmities— Mary called Magdalene... and many others who provided for Him from their substance."* (Luke 8:1-3, NKJV)
- *"Then they returned from the tomb and told all these things to the eleven and to all the rest. It was Mary Magdalene, Joanna, Mary the mother of James, and the other women with them, who told these things to the apostles."* (Luke 24:9-10, NKJV)

Key Points

- **Jesus Spoke Directly to Women** In a time when women were often ignored, Jesus initiated conversations, showing that they were worthy of His attention and teaching.
- **Women Were Among Jesus' Disciples** Luke 8 describes how women traveled with Jesus and supported His ministry, demonstrating their active participation.
- **Jesus Defended Women Against Cultural Judgment** When the woman anointed His feet with oil, He silenced those who criticized her and publicly honored her devotion.
- **He Entrusted Women With the Resurrection Message** The first witnesses of the empty tomb were women, chosen by Jesus to proclaim the greatest news in history.
- **Jesus Healed and Restored Women** From the woman with the issue of blood to the daughter of Jairus, Jesus healed not only physically but emotionally and socially.
- **He Challenged Cultural Norms** When Jesus spoke with the Samaritan woman at the well, He broke multiple cultural barriers to offer her salvation and purpose.
- **Jesus' Actions Set a Standard for the Church** If Jesus honored, taught, and empowered women, the church must follow His example rather than cultural traditions that restrict them.

Journaling Questions

Journaling allows us to evaluate whether our personal views align with Jesus' example. Have you fully embraced how Jesus uplifted and honored women, or have cultural assumptions influenced your perspective? Reflect on moments when Jesus' interactions with women challenged societal norms and what that means for today.

As you answer the following questions, consider how Jesus' heart toward women should shape your own beliefs and actions.

Recognizing Jesus' Example

Which of Jesus' interactions with women stands out most to you, and why?

_____
_____
_____
_____
_____
_____
_____

Aligning With His Heart

Are there any ways in which you have unknowingly adopted cultural biases that contradict Jesus' treatment of women?

_____
_____
_____
_____
_____
_____
_____

The Role of Women in Ministry

How do Jesus' actions affirm the value of women serving in ministry today?

_____
_____
_____
_____
_____
_____
_____

Applying His Example

What steps can you take to ensure that your attitudes and actions toward women reflect Jesus' heart?

_____
_____
_____
_____
_____
_____

Empowering Others

How can you support and encourage women in their calling within the church and beyond?

_____
_____
_____
_____
_____
_____

Actionable Steps

Cultivate a Christ-Like Perspective
Study Jesus' interactions with women and allow His example to reshape any areas of misunderstanding or bias.

Equip Yourself With Biblical Knowledge
Learn more about the historical and cultural context of Jesus' time to better appreciate how radical His treatment of women was.

Engage in Practical Advocacy
Actively support women in ministry by affirming their calling, providing opportunities, and challenging restrictions that contradict Jesus' model.

Personal Reflection

Jesus never diminished or dismissed women—He embraced, taught, and empowered them. If we are to follow Him, we must do the same. Have you allowed His example to fully shape your understanding of women in the church, or have traditions influenced your perspective?

If Jesus entrusted women with the message of His resurrection, how can we deny them the right to proclaim His Word today? The heart of Christ is not one of exclusion but of calling and commissioning. Will you align with His heart?

If Jesus honored, taught, and empowered women, what should our response be? How will you reflect His example in your own life?

Closing Prayer: *Lord, thank You for revealing Your heart toward women through Jesus' life and ministry. Help me to see through Your eyes, breaking free from any perspectives that contradict Your truth. May I honor, support, and empower those You have called, just as You did. Let my life reflect Your love and justice. In Jesus' name, Amen.*

Chapter 6

Prophecies Regarding Last-Days Women

"And it shall come to pass afterward that I will pour out My Spirit on all flesh; your sons and your daughters shall prophesy, your old men shall dream dreams, your young men shall see visions." (Joel 2:28, NKJV)

She stood in the middle of the gathering, her hands trembling as she lifted her voice to speak. The words flowed, not from her own thoughts, but from the Spirit of God stirring within her. As she prophesied, some listened in awe, while others whispered among themselves, questioning whether God would truly use a woman in such a way. Yet, the undeniable presence of the Holy Spirit silenced doubt, confirming that God was speaking through her.

Throughout history, women have been pivotal in prophetic movements, yet their role has often been questioned or dismissed. However, Scripture is clear—God has always used women as prophetic voices. From Miriam and Deborah to Anna and Philip's daughters, women have played a vital role in delivering divine messages. The prophecy of Joel, echoed by Peter on the day of Pentecost, confirms that in the last days, God will pour out His Spirit on both men and women, empowering them to prophesy.

Despite this clear biblical precedent, many still struggle with the idea of women carrying prophetic authority. Some dismiss their voices, while others limit their influence. But if God Himself declared that daughters would prophesy, who are we to silence them? The last-days outpouring of the Spirit is not gender-specific—it is a movement of God that calls all His people to speak His Word boldly.

This chapter challenges us to embrace God's prophetic plan for women in the last days. If Scripture proclaims that daughters will prophesy, are we willing to listen?

Focus Point

"On My menservants and on My maidservants I will pour out My Spirit in those days; and they shall prophesy." (Acts 2:18, NKJV)

This verse, spoken by Peter on the day of Pentecost, affirms that the Holy Spirit empowers both men and women to prophesy. It confirms that spiritual gifts are not limited by gender but are given according to God's purpose.

Main Theme

Defining your relationship with Jesus begins with understanding His relentless pursuit of you. He's not looking for a casual fling or a part-time companion. He's seeking a bride who is wholly devoted and ready to embrace His love fully. Just as a bridegroom takes great risks to win his bride, Jesus risked everything to redeem us. The call to define your relationship with Him is not just an emotional decision; it's a life-altering covenant.

"Jesus is pursuing you—now it's time to define your relationship with Him."

Key Scriptures

- *"And it shall come to pass afterward that I will pour out My Spirit on all flesh; your sons and your daughters shall prophesy, your old men shall dream dreams, your young men shall see visions."* (Joel 2:28, NKJV)
- *"Now this man had four virgin daughters who prophesied."* (Acts 21:9, NKJV)
- *"Then the angel of the Lord said to her, 'Return to your mistress, and submit yourself under her hand.' Then the angel of the Lord said to her, 'I will multiply your descendants exceedingly, so that they shall not be counted for multitude.'"* (Genesis 16:9-10, NKJV)

Key Points

- **The Holy Spirit Is Poured Out on All People** Joel's prophecy makes it clear that the last-days revival includes both men and women operating in spiritual gifts.
- **Women Have Always Been Prophetic Voices** From Miriam in the Old Testament to Philip's daughters in the New Testament, Scripture records women serving as prophets.
- **God's Call Overrides Human Tradition** Many cultures have sought to suppress women's voices in ministry, but God's call transcends cultural limitations.
- **The Early Church Recognized Female Prophets** Acts 21:9 highlights that Philip's daughters were known for their prophetic gifting, demonstrating that women were active in ministry.
- **Prophecy Is Not Gender-Specific** If prophecy were meant only for men, Scripture would not repeatedly affirm that both sons and daughters will prophesy.
- **God Calls and Equips Whom He Chooses** When God anoints someone to speak His Word, human barriers and traditions cannot stand against His purpose.
- **The Church Must Align With God's Plan** To fulfill the last-days prophetic movement, the church must embrace the biblical truth that women are called to prophesy.

Journaling Questions

Journaling allows us to process our beliefs about God's prophetic calling on women. Have you ever struggled with the idea of women prophesying or leading in ministry? If so, where did those beliefs originate? Scripture calls us to renew our minds according to God's truth, not human traditions.

Through reflection, you can identify any areas where tradition has influenced your views more than Scripture. Allow the Holy Spirit to speak as you consider how God is calling both men and women to proclaim His Word in these last days.

Understanding Prophetic Calling

How does Joel's prophecy challenge traditional views on women in ministry?

Biblical Examples

What stands out to you about the women in the Bible who were recognized as prophets?

Recognizing God's Anointing

Have you seen evidence of God's Spirit moving through women in prophetic ministry? How has it impacted your faith?

Aligning With Scripture

Are there any traditional beliefs or cultural assumptions you need to surrender in order to fully embrace God's calling for women?

_____
_____
_____
_____
_____
_____
_____

Supporting Women in Ministry

What practical steps can you take to encourage and support women who are called to prophesy?

_____
_____
_____
_____
_____
_____
_____

Actionable Steps

Cultivate an Open Heart to God's Call
Study Joel 2:28 and Acts 2:18 with a willingness to embrace what God says about women in prophetic ministry.

Equip Yourself With Biblical Truth
Examine historical and biblical accounts of women who prophesied and share this knowledge with others.

Engage in Encouragement and Advocacy
Support women who are called to ministry by affirming their gifts, providing opportunities, and challenging restrictions that contradict Scripture.

Personal Reflection

The prophecy of Joel is a powerful declaration of God's intention for the last-days church. He has made it clear that both sons and daughters will prophesy, yet many still resist this truth. Have you fully embraced the prophetic calling of women, or have cultural beliefs influenced your perspective?

If the Holy Spirit is moving in these last days, we must align ourselves with His plan. The church cannot afford to silence those whom God has called. Will you stand with the prophetic voices God is raising up?

If God has declared that daughters will prophesy, how will you respond? Will you listen, support, and make room for them to fulfill His calling?

Closing Prayer: *Lord, thank You for pouring out Your Spirit on all flesh. Help me to fully embrace Your calling on both men and women in these last days. Remove any biases that hinder Your work, and let me be a vessel of encouragement and support for those You have anointed. May Your prophetic voices rise up boldly to proclaim Your truth. In Jesus' name, Amen.*

Chapter 7

Paul and Women

"Greet Andronicus and Junia, my countrymen and my fellow prisoners, who are of note among the apostles, who also were in Christ before me." (Romans 16:7, NKJV)

She hesitated before speaking, her voice filled with uncertainty. "I know God calls women, but what about Paul? Didn't he say women should be silent?" It was a question I had heard many times before, often accompanied by a sense of frustration or resignation. For centuries, certain verses from Paul's letters have been used to limit women's roles in ministry. But were Paul's words truly meant to silence women permanently, or have they been misunderstood?

Paul's relationship with women in ministry was far more complex than the restrictive interpretations often presented. He honored women as co-laborers, entrusted them with leadership, and acknowledged their work in spreading the gospel. From Priscilla, who taught Apollos, to Junia, noted as an apostle, Paul's letters contain multiple affirmations of women serving alongside men in key roles.

Yet, some of Paul's writings, particularly 1 Corinthians 14:34-35 and 1 Timothy 2:11-12, seem to contradict his support of women in ministry. How do we reconcile these passages with his clear endorsement of female leaders? The answer lies in understanding Paul's cultural context, the issues he was addressing, and his overarching commitment to the gospel's advancement.

This chapter invites us to take a closer look at Paul's words, not in isolation, but within the full scope of Scripture. If Paul truly championed women in ministry, are we willing to embrace his full message rather than selective restrictions?

Focus Point

"There is neither Jew nor Greek, there is neither slave nor free, there is neither male nor female; for you are all one in Christ Jesus." (Galatians 3:28, NKJV)

This verse is a cornerstone of Paul's teaching, affirming that in Christ, all barriers—including gender—are removed. The gospel restores equality, emphasizing spiritual unity and shared purpose in the Kingdom.

Main Theme

Paul's letters reveal a profound respect for women in ministry. While some passages have been used to restrict women, a closer examination shows that Paul consistently affirmed their role in leadership and teaching. His words must be interpreted in the full context of his writings, cultural background, and the biblical narrative of God's calling.

"Paul did not silence women—he empowered them."

Key Scriptures

- *"Greet Andronicus and Junia, my countrymen and my fellow prisoners, who are of note among the apostles, who also were in Christ before me."* (Romans 16:7, NKJV)
- *"I commend to you Phoebe our sister, who is a servant of the church in Cenchrea."* (Romans 16:1, NKJV)
- *"Likewise, greet the church that is in their house. Greet my beloved Epaenetus, who is the firstfruits of Achaia to Christ."* (Romans 16:5, NKJV)

Key Points

- **Paul Recognized Women as Apostles and Leaders** Junia is explicitly named as an apostle, signifying a high-ranking leadership role in the early church.
- **Women Were Among Paul's Trusted Co-Laborers** Phoebe, Priscilla, and others were commended by Paul as valuable leaders and ministers of the gospel.

- **Paul Advocated for Unity in Christ** Galatians 3:28 affirms that all believers, regardless of gender, are one in Christ and share in the work of the Kingdom.
- **Cultural Context Matters in Interpretation** Paul's instructions regarding women's silence were specific to certain cultural and situational issues, not universal restrictions.
- **Paul Encouraged Women to Teach** Priscilla, alongside her husband Aquila, was recognized as a teacher who instructed Apollos in the way of God.
- **Silence in 1 Corinthians 14 Was About Order, Not Restriction** The command for women to be silent was addressing disorderly conduct in Corinth, not prohibiting them from speaking altogether.
- **The Gospel Always Expands Opportunity, Not Limits It** Jesus and Paul both elevated women's roles rather than diminishing them, aligning with God's redemptive work throughout history.

Journaling Questions

Journaling allows us to explore how our understanding of Paul's writings has been shaped. Have you ever struggled with reconciling Paul's words with his actions? If so, what has influenced your perspective? Scripture calls us to seek truth, not tradition, as our foundation.

Through reflection, you may uncover areas where long-held beliefs have been influenced more by cultural interpretation than biblical truth. Allow God's Word to reshape your understanding as you consider Paul's full message.

Understanding Paul's Intent

How does knowing Paul affirmed women in ministry change your perspective on his writings?

_____
_____
_____
_____
_____
_____
_____

Examining Key Figures

What stands out to you about Junia, Phoebe, and Priscilla in Paul's letters?

_____
_____
_____
_____
_____
_____

Addressing Difficult Passages

How does understanding cultural context help clarify Paul's instructions on women's roles?

_____
_____
_____
_____
_____
_____

Personal Reflection

Have you ever struggled with how Paul's writings have been used to limit women? If so, how has your view evolved?

_____
_____
_____
_____
_____
_____

Aligning With Scripture

What steps can you take to ensure your beliefs about women in ministry align with the full biblical narrative?

_____
_____
_____
_____
_____

Actionable Steps

Cultivate a Contextual Understanding of Scripture
Study Paul's letters with historical and cultural awareness, seeking to grasp his full intent.

Equip Yourself With Biblical Knowledge
Examine how women were actively involved in Paul's ministry and compare that with restrictive interpretations.

Engage in Advocacy and Support
Encourage and support women who are called to leadership by affirming their biblical right to serve.

Personal Reflection

Paul's writings have been misused to restrict women, yet his actions paint a different picture—one of affirmation and empowerment. If we are to interpret Scripture rightly, we must consider Paul's entire message rather than isolated verses. Are you willing to reassess long-held beliefs in light of the full biblical narrative?

God has never been in the business of silencing those He calls. Paul himself acknowledged and worked alongside women in ministry, affirming their place in the mission of Christ. Will you embrace this truth?

If Paul empowered women in ministry, how should that influence our view today? Are we willing to align with his full message rather than selective restrictions?

Closing Prayer: Lord, thank You for the truth of Your Word and for calling both men and women to serve in Your Kingdom. Help me to see beyond tradition and embrace the full picture of Your calling. May I honor and support those You have anointed, just as Paul did. Let my understanding be shaped by Your truth alone. In Jesus' name, Amen.

Chapter 8

Who May Minister?

"There is neither Jew nor Greek, there is neither slave nor free, there is neither male nor female; for you are all one in Christ Jesus." (Galatians 3:28, NKJV)

She sat in the back of the church, watching the preacher with a mixture of longing and uncertainty. Her heart burned with the desire to share God's Word, yet she had been told time and again that ministry was not for her. "You can serve," they said, "but leave the preaching to the men." The conflict within her grew as she wrestled with the question: *Does God truly call both men and women to minister?*

The question of who may minister has been debated for centuries, often shaped more by tradition than by Scripture. Some argue that ministry is reserved for men, while others recognize the biblical evidence of women called, anointed, and commissioned by God. Throughout both the Old and New Testaments, God has consistently used those whom He chooses—regardless of gender—to carry out His divine purpose.

Jesus' ministry shattered cultural expectations, empowering those whom society had overlooked. The early church continued this pattern, embracing both men and women as ministers of the gospel. If God calls, equips, and anoints, then who are we to determine who may or may not minister in His name?

This chapter challenges us to align our beliefs with Scripture, not tradition. If God's Spirit is poured out on all people, then ministry must be open to all whom He calls. Are we willing to embrace the fullness of God's design?

Focus Point

"And He Himself gave some to be apostles, some prophets, some evangelists, and some pastors and teachers." (Ephesians 4:11, NKJV)

This verse affirms that ministry gifts are given by Christ Himself. The passage does not specify gender because God's calling is not based on human distinctions but on His divine purpose.

Main Theme

Ministry is not determined by gender, social status, or cultural norms—it is determined by God's call. The Bible provides numerous examples of both men and women ministering effectively under God's anointing. To restrict ministry based on gender is to place human limitations on a divine commission.

"When God calls, He equips—without restriction."

Key Scriptures

- *"There is neither Jew nor Greek, there is neither slave nor free, there is neither male nor female; for you are all one in Christ Jesus."* (Galatians 3:28, NKJV)
- *"I commend to you Phoebe our sister, who is a servant of the church in Cenchrea."* (Romans 16:1, NKJV)
- *"And on My menservants and on My maidservants I will pour out My Spirit in those days; and they shall prophesy."* (Acts 2:18, NKJV)

Key Points

- **God Calls Whom He Chooses** Scripture is filled with examples of God calling people to ministry without regard to gender, including Deborah, Priscilla, and Phoebe.
- **The Great Commission Is for All Believers** Jesus instructed all His followers—men and women—to go and make disciples, preach, and teach.

- **Ministry Gifts Are Given by Christ** Ephesians 4:11 states that Jesus Himself gave ministry gifts, making no distinction between male and female.
- **The Early Church Included Women in Ministry** Romans 16 highlights several women who held leadership roles, confirming that women were active in ministry.
- **The Holy Spirit Empowers All People** Joel 2:28 and Acts 2:18 affirm that both men and women will prophesy under the power of the Holy Spirit.
- **Jesus Broke Cultural Barriers** He engaged with, taught, and empowered women, demonstrating that ministry is not confined to gender roles.
- **Ministry Is About Calling, Not Tradition** Human traditions should never override God's Word. If He calls a woman, she is fully qualified to serve.

Journaling Questions

Journaling allows us to process whether our views on ministry align with Scripture or tradition. Have you ever questioned who may serve in ministry? Have cultural influences shaped your perspective more than biblical truth? Scripture invites us to examine and align our understanding with God's revealed Word.

As you reflect on these questions, ask God to remove any biases or misconceptions and replace them with His truth.

Examining the Call

Have you ever felt a calling to ministry? If so, how have you responded to it?

_____
_____
_____
_____
_____
_____
_____

Biblical Evidence

What examples from Scripture affirm that both men and women can minister?

Breaking Barriers

Have you ever witnessed a woman being discouraged from ministry? How did it impact you?

Aligning With God's Truth

Are there any traditional beliefs you need to let go of in order to embrace God's full design for ministry?

Encouraging Others

How can you support those whom God has called to ministry, regardless of gender?

_____
_____
_____
_____
_____
_____

Actionable Steps

Cultivate a Biblical Perspective
Study passages that highlight women in ministry and compare them with common interpretations that limit their roles.

Equip Yourself With Truth
Engage in discussions and teachings that align with Scripture's affirmation of God's calling for all believers.

Engage in Supportive Action
Encourage and affirm those who are called to ministry, advocating for their rightful place in the Body of Christ.

Personal Reflection

The question of who may minister is ultimately a question of obedience to God's call. If He anoints someone for ministry, no human tradition should stand in the way. Have you allowed Scripture to shape your beliefs, or have cultural traditions influenced your perspective?

God's Spirit is moving in these last days, calling both men and women to serve in His Kingdom. The church must align with His plan, making room for those He has anointed. Will you support those He has called?

If God calls and equips without restriction, how will you respond? Will you affirm His work in all whom He has chosen?

Closing Prayer: *Lord, thank You for calling both men and women to minister in Your Kingdom. Help me to see beyond tradition and embrace the fullness of Your design. Remove any barriers that limit those You have anointed, and let me be an encourager to those who are stepping into their calling. May Your Spirit move freely in the lives of all whom You have chosen. In Jesus' name, Amen.*

Chapter 9

"Let the Woman Learn in Silence"

"Let a woman learn in silence with all submission. And I do not permit a woman to teach or to have authority over a man, but to be in silence." (1 Timothy 2:11-12, NKJV)

She had spent years faithfully studying the Word, feeling the call of God stirring within her. But every time she shared her desire to minister, she was met with a familiar response: *"Women should be silent in the church."* It was a verse she had heard quoted often, but deep inside, she wondered—was that truly what Paul meant? Had God really called her only to have His own Word silence her?

Many women have faced this same struggle. For centuries, 1 Timothy 2:11-12 has been used as a definitive statement against women in ministry. Yet, when examined within its cultural and historical context, we find that Paul's words were addressing a specific issue, not issuing a universal command for all time. The same Paul who wrote these words also commended women as co-laborers, teachers, and leaders within the early church.

If we are to understand Scripture rightly, we must examine the full biblical picture rather than extracting isolated verses. Did Paul intend to silence all women, or was he addressing a specific problem in a specific church? And more importantly, what does God's overall Word say about women learning, teaching, and ministering?

This chapter invites us to step beyond surface-level interpretations and seek the heart of God. Are we willing to dig deeper and uncover the full truth?

Focus Point

"There is neither Jew nor Greek, there is neither slave nor free, there is neither male nor female; for you are all one in Christ Jesus." (Galatians 3:28, NKJV)

This verse reminds us that in Christ, all believers—regardless of gender—share equal standing in salvation and service. Any interpretation of Paul's writings that contradicts the unity and inclusion of the gospel must be carefully reconsidered.

Main Theme

The command for women to learn in silence was not a universal prohibition against women in ministry, but a specific instruction given within a cultural and historical context. The full testimony of Scripture affirms that God calls, equips, and anoints women to teach, lead, and minister.

"God does not contradict Himself—He calls whom He chooses, and His gifts are without repentance."

Key Scriptures

- *"Let a woman learn in silence with all submission. And I do not permit a woman to teach or to have authority over a man, but to be in silence."* (1 Timothy 2:11-12, NKJV)
- *"I commend to you Phoebe our sister, who is a servant of the church in Cenchrea."* (Romans 16:1, NKJV)
- *"Priscilla and Aquila took him aside and explained to him the way of God more accurately."* (Acts 18:26, NKJV)

Key Points

- **Paul Was Addressing a Specific Cultural Issue** The church in Ephesus, where Timothy was ministering, struggled with false teaching, and some untrained women were spreading misinformation.

- **Silence Was a Temporary Corrective Measure** Paul's command for silence was not an eternal mandate but a situational directive to address disorder and improper teaching.
- **Paul Supported Women in Ministry** Throughout his letters, Paul affirmed female leaders, including Priscilla, Phoebe, and Junia, demonstrating that he did not universally silence women.
- **Women Were Encouraged to Learn** In a time when women had little access to education, Paul's instruction for them to learn was actually revolutionary and empowering.
- **The Greek Word for "Authority" Matters** The word translated as "authority" (*authentein*) in 1 Timothy 2:12 is a rare term, meaning "to dominate or control aggressively," not simply "to lead."
- **Context Always Determines Interpretation** Interpreting Scripture requires considering its historical, cultural, and literary context. A single verse should never override the full biblical narrative.
- **God's Calling Is Not Limited by Gender** If God calls a woman to teach, preach, or lead, human traditions should not stand in opposition to His divine will.

Journaling Questions

Journaling allows us to evaluate how Scripture has shaped our views on women in ministry. Have you ever struggled with this passage in 1 Timothy? Have you been taught a restrictive interpretation without considering historical context?

Reflecting on these questions can help uncover areas where tradition may have influenced our understanding more than Scripture itself. Seek God's truth with an open heart and allow the Holy Spirit to reveal His perspective.

Understanding Paul's Words

How does knowing the historical context of 1 Timothy 2:11-12 affect your understanding of Paul's intent?

_____
_____
_____
_____

Exploring Biblical Examples

What do the examples of Priscilla, Phoebe, and Junia reveal about Paul's view of women in ministry?

Challenging Assumptions

Have you ever accepted a restrictive interpretation of this passage without fully studying it? If so, what led you to believe it?

Recognizing God's Call

If God has called and anointed women throughout history, how should that influence our view of women in the church today?

Aligning With God's Word

What steps can you take to ensure that your beliefs about women in ministry align with the full biblical narrative rather than isolated verses?

_____
_____
_____
_____
_____
_____

Actionable Steps

Cultivate Biblical Understanding
Commit to studying the full context of difficult passages, ensuring that your interpretations align with God's overall message.

Equip Yourself With Historical Knowledge
Research the cultural and linguistic background of 1 Timothy to gain a clearer understanding of Paul's words.

Engage in Support and Advocacy
Encourage women who are called to ministry by affirming their gifts and helping to remove barriers that hinder their service.

Personal Reflection

The call of God cannot be silenced by misinterpretation. If we are to be faithful to Scripture, we must examine it in its full context rather than relying on traditions that limit God's work. Are you willing to let go of restrictive interpretations and embrace the biblical truth of God's calling?

God has called and anointed women throughout history to teach, lead, and minister. If Paul himself recognized and worked alongside these women, why should we stand in opposition to their calling? Will you support those whom God has chosen?

If God calls and anoints, who are we to silence His chosen vessels? Will you stand for the full truth of His Word?

Closing Prayer: *Lord, thank You for the truth of Your Word, which sets us free. Help me to seek understanding and wisdom as I study difficult passages. Remove any barriers that keep me from fully embracing Your calling for all believers. May I be a voice of affirmation and support for those whom You have anointed. In Jesus' name, Amen.*

Chapter 10

"It Is Not Permitted unto Them to Speak"

"Let your women keep silent in the churches, for they are not permitted to speak; but they are to be submissive, as the law also says." (1 Corinthians 14:34, NKJV)

She sat quietly, hesitant to raise her hand during the Bible study. For years, she had heard 1 Corinthians 14:34 quoted as an absolute rule—women should remain silent in the church. But deep inside, she wrestled with questions: *Was Paul truly forbidding all women from speaking? If so, how do we reconcile that with the many women in Scripture who prophesied, taught, and led?*

This verse has long been used as a definitive statement against women speaking in church, but does it truly mean what many assume? Paul, the same apostle who affirmed women as prophets and co-laborers in the gospel, would seemingly be contradicting himself if this verse were taken as an absolute, universal prohibition. Understanding the context of this passage is crucial to grasping Paul's intent.

In Corinth, the church was experiencing disorderly worship, with interruptions, chaotic speaking, and confusion. Paul's instruction for women to remain silent must be read in light of this broader concern. Rather than restricting all women from speaking in every church context, Paul was addressing a specific problem of disruptive behavior.

This chapter challenges us to read Scripture carefully, seeking the heart of God rather than settling for surface-level interpretations. If God has called and anointed women to proclaim His Word, how can we interpret this verse in a way that aligns with His greater biblical narrative?

Focus Point

"For God is not the author of confusion but of peace, as in all the churches of the saints." (1 Corinthians 14:33, NKJV)

This verse immediately precedes Paul's instruction about silence, showing that his concern was about order in worship, not restricting women from speaking entirely. God's design for the church is one of peace, not division or suppression.

Main Theme

Paul's command for women to be silent in 1 Corinthians 14 was not a universal prohibition against women speaking, but a corrective measure addressing disorder in worship. Throughout Scripture, God uses women to teach, prophesy, and lead, proving that their voices are not forbidden but valued in His Kingdom.

"God's order brings clarity, not restriction."

Key Scriptures

- *"Let your women keep silent in the churches, for they are not permitted to speak; but they are to be submissive, as the law also says."* (1 Corinthians 14:34, NKJV)
- *"Every woman who prays or prophesies with her head uncovered dishonors her head."* (1 Corinthians 11:5, NKJV)
- *"And on My menservants and on My maidservants I will pour out My Spirit in those days; and they shall prophesy."* (Acts 2:18, NKJV)

Key Points

- **Paul Was Addressing a Specific Issue in Corinth** The Corinthian church was experiencing chaotic gatherings, and Paul's instruction aimed to restore order, not permanently silence women.

- **Women Were Already Speaking in Church** In 1 Corinthians 11:5, Paul acknowledges that women were prophesying in church, proving that he did not intend an absolute prohibition.
- **The Greek Word for 'Silent' Can Mean 'Peaceful'** The word translated as "silent" (*sigao*) in Greek often means to be peaceful or refrain from disorderly interruptions.
- **The Reference to the Law Is Unclear** There is no known Mosaic law that forbids women from speaking, indicating that Paul was likely addressing local customs rather than a biblical command.
- **Paul Commended Women in Ministry** Throughout his letters, Paul affirmed the roles of women like Phoebe, Priscilla, and Junia, showing that he did not universally restrict women from speaking.
- **Cultural Context Influences Interpretation** In the first-century Greco-Roman world, women were often uneducated and learning for the first time in church settings, requiring temporary instruction on conduct.
- **God Calls and Anoints Without Gender Restrictions** Joel 2:28 and Acts 2:18 affirm that both men and women will prophesy under the power of the Holy Spirit, showing that their voices are meant to be heard.

Journaling Questions

Journaling allows us to process whether our understanding of this passage aligns with the full message of Scripture. Have you ever struggled with reconciling this verse with the broader biblical affirmation of women in ministry? What influences have shaped your view of women speaking in church?

Understanding the Context

How does knowing the cultural background of 1 Corinthians 14 affect your understanding of Paul's instruction?

_____
_____
_____
_____

Reconciling Other Passages

If Paul allowed women to prophesy in 1 Corinthians 11, why do you think he instructed silence in chapter 14?

_____
_____
_____
_____
_____
_____

Recognizing Misinterpretations

Have you ever accepted a restrictive view of this passage without fully studying it? What led you to that belief?

_____
_____
_____
_____
_____
_____

God's Calling on Women

Do you believe God calls and equips both men and women to speak His Word? Why or why not?

_____
_____
_____
_____
_____

Aligning With Scripture

What steps can you take to ensure your understanding of women speaking in church aligns with the full biblical narrative?

_____
_____
_____
_____
_____
_____

Actionable Steps

Cultivate a Holistic Understanding of Scripture
Commit to studying the broader context of passages that have been used to restrict women, ensuring your beliefs align with the entire biblical message.

Equip Yourself With Historical Knowledge
Research first-century church culture to better understand the issues Paul was addressing in Corinth.

Engage in Encouragement and Support
Affirm and support women who are called to teach and speak in church, helping to remove barriers that misinterpret Scripture.

Personal Reflection

The gospel is a message of freedom, restoration, and calling. If we take isolated verses and use them to suppress those whom God has anointed, we risk distorting His Word. Are you willing to examine Scripture more deeply to uncover the full truth?

Throughout history, God has called women to be messengers of His truth. If Paul himself recognized and worked alongside women in ministry, should we not do the same? Will you support and affirm the voices that God has empowered?

If God has given His Spirit to both men and women, why would He restrict those He has called? Will you stand for the full truth of His Word?

_____
_____
_____
_____
_____
_____
_____
_____
_____
_____
_____
_____
_____
_____
_____
_____
_____
_____
_____
_____
_____
_____
_____
_____
_____

Closing Prayer: *Lord, thank You for Your Word, which brings truth and freedom. Help me to seek understanding and wisdom as I study difficult passages. Let me recognize and affirm those whom You have called to proclaim Your message. May I be a voice of encouragement, not restriction, and may I always align my beliefs with Your truth. In Jesus' name, Amen.*

Chapter 11

How Did We Get Here?

"You have made the commandment of God of no effect by your tradition." (Matthew 15:6, NKJV)

She sat in the pew, listening to another sermon that subtly reinforced the idea that women should remain in the background. She had never questioned it before—it was simply the way things had always been. But something stirred within her. *How did we get here?* she wondered. *How did the church, which was meant to reflect Christ's love and equality, come to silence half of its members?*

The suppression of women in ministry was not part of God's original design. From the beginning, Scripture reveals God calling both men and women to lead, prophesy, and serve. Yet over time, human traditions, cultural biases, and misinterpretations of Scripture have shaped a church culture that often restricts women's voices. Many of these restrictions have little to do with biblical truth and more to do with societal norms that crept into church teachings over the centuries.

Church history reveals a long journey—one filled with moments of inclusion and empowerment, but also periods of exclusion and misunderstanding. The question is, will we continue following human tradition, or will we return to the truth of God's Word? The time has come to examine how we arrived at this point and, more importantly, how we can realign with God's true intent for His people.

This chapter invites us to question the status quo and rediscover God's original plan. Are we willing to challenge centuries of tradition in order to embrace biblical truth?

Focus Point

"Therefore if the Son makes you free, you shall be free indeed." (John 8:36, NKJV)

Jesus came to bring freedom—not just from sin, but from every form of bondage, including the restrictions placed on those He has called. Any church tradition that contradicts the freedom Christ offers must be re-examined in light of Scripture.

Main Theme

The restrictions placed on women in ministry are largely the result of human traditions rather than divine mandates. Throughout Scripture and history, God has called both men and women to serve. The church must return to God's original design and reject traditions that contradict His Word.

"God's calling is not confined by human tradition."

Key Scriptures

- *"You have made the commandment of God of no effect by your tradition."* (Matthew 15:6, NKJV)
- *"There is neither Jew nor Greek, there is neither slave nor free, there is neither male nor female; for you are all one in Christ Jesus."* (Galatians 3:28, NKJV)
- *"And I will pour out My Spirit on all flesh; your sons and your daughters shall prophesy."* (Joel 2:28, NKJV)

Key Points

- **The Early Church Embraced Women in Ministry** Women played vital roles in the early church, serving as apostles, prophets, teachers, and leaders.
- **Cultural Influence Distorted Biblical Teaching** As the church expanded, cultural norms from patriarchal societies influenced the interpretation and application of Scripture.

- **The Middle Ages Further Restricted Women** During this period, women were increasingly excluded from leadership roles, reinforcing male-dominated church structures.
- **The Reformation Revived the Question** Although the Reformation emphasized Scripture, many reformers maintained traditional restrictions on women despite biblical evidence of their callings.
- **Modern Movements Have Challenged These Traditions** In the last two centuries, women have increasingly stepped into ministry, rediscovering biblical support for their roles.
- **The Holy Spirit Empowers All Believers** Joel 2:28 confirms that God pours out His Spirit on both men and women, empowering them to speak His Word.
- **Returning to Biblical Truth Requires Courage** Challenging centuries of tradition is not easy, but obedience to God's Word is more important than maintaining human customs.

Journaling Questions

Journaling allows us to reflect on how history, tradition, and Scripture have shaped our views on women in ministry. Have you ever accepted certain church traditions without questioning their biblical foundation? Have you considered how culture has influenced your perspective more than Scripture?

Through reflection, you can identify areas where you may need to realign with God's truth. Seek the Holy Spirit's guidance in discerning whether your beliefs about women in ministry are rooted in God's Word or human tradition.

Examining Church Tradition

What are some beliefs about women in ministry that you have accepted without fully studying Scripture?

_____
_____
_____
_____
_____

Recognizing Cultural Influence

How have societal norms throughout history influenced the church's stance on women in leadership?

Understanding Biblical Freedom

How does Jesus' message of freedom challenge the restrictions placed on women in ministry?

Personal Reflection

Have you ever struggled with embracing the idea that God calls women to minister? What led you to that struggle?

Aligning With Truth

What steps can you take to ensure that your beliefs about ministry align with God's Word rather than tradition?

_____
_____
_____
_____
_____
_____

Actionable Steps

Cultivate a Biblical Perspective
Commit to studying the full scope of Scripture regarding women in ministry, seeking God's truth above human tradition.

Equip Yourself With Historical Knowledge
Research how church history has influenced perspectives on women and compare that with biblical teachings.

Engage in Advocacy and Encouragement
Support and affirm women who are called to ministry, helping to remove barriers that are based on tradition rather than Scripture.

Personal Reflection

Understanding how we arrived at this point is essential to moving forward in God's truth. The suppression of women in ministry was not God's plan—it was shaped by cultural traditions that the church adopted over time. Are you willing to re-examine these traditions in light of God's Word?

If God has called and anointed both men and women, then any teaching that restricts ministry based on gender must be questioned. Will you stand for the full truth of Scripture, even when it challenges long-held traditions?

If Jesus came to set us free, why would we allow tradition to keep us in bondage? Will you embrace His truth over human customs?

Closing Prayer: *Lord, thank You for revealing truth and calling all Your people to serve in Your Kingdom. Help me to discern between Your commands and human traditions. Give me the courage to embrace and support those You have anointed, regardless of gender. Let my life be a reflection of Your truth, free from the limitations of culture and tradition. In Jesus' name, Amen.*

Chapter 12

Free to Answer His Call

"If the Son makes you free, you shall be free indeed." (John 8:36, NKJV)

She had spent years believing that her desire to teach and lead in the church was misplaced. Every time she felt the stirring in her spirit, she reminded herself of the voices that had told her, "God calls women to serve, but not to lead." Yet, no matter how much she tried to suppress it, the call of God remained. One day, as she read through Scripture, she saw something she had never noticed before—God had always called women. Deborah, Esther, Mary Magdalene, and Priscilla had all played pivotal roles in His Kingdom. Could it be that she, too, was truly free to answer His call?

For centuries, women have struggled under restrictions that were never part of God's original plan. The weight of tradition has often silenced those whom God has chosen, but His calling remains unshaken. Jesus Himself demonstrated a revolutionary approach—affirming, teaching, and commissioning women in ways that defied cultural norms. The early church followed His example, recognizing women as prophets, teachers, and leaders.

Yet, many today still wrestle with doubt, wondering if they are truly free to step into the calling God has placed on their lives. This chapter invites us to embrace the full freedom Christ offers and to reject any limitation that contradicts His will. If God calls, anoints, and equips, who are we to say no?

The question remains: Will you step forward in faith and answer His call?

Focus Point

"For God has not given us a spirit of fear, but of power and of love and of a sound mind." (2 Timothy 1:7, NKJV)

God's calling is never accompanied by fear, only by the power and confidence that comes from knowing He has equipped us for the task. Fear is not from God; courage is.

Main Theme

Jesus came to break every chain, including the chains of limitation placed upon those He has called. His freedom extends to every believer, regardless of gender. If He calls you, He will equip you. The only question is whether you will walk in the freedom He has given you.

"God's call is not limited by human opinion—it is confirmed by His anointing."

Key Scriptures

- *"If the Son makes you free, you shall be free indeed."* (John 8:36, NKJV)
- *"There is neither Jew nor Greek, there is neither slave nor free, there is neither male nor female; for you are all one in Christ Jesus."* (Galatians 3:28, NKJV)
- *"But the manifestation of the Spirit is given to each one for the profit of all."* (1 Corinthians 12:7, NKJV)

Key Points

- **Jesus Came to Set Us Free** The restrictions placed on women in ministry are not from God, but from human traditions that Jesus came to break.
- **Freedom Is Found in Christ, Not in Tradition** If Christ has set us free, then no man-made rule or cultural expectation can take that freedom away.
- **The Holy Spirit Equips Whom He Calls** Spiritual gifts are distributed according to God's will, not human limitations, meaning that women are just as equipped as men to minister.

- **The Early Church Affirmed Women in Ministry** From Priscilla to Junia, Scripture confirms that women played vital roles in the growth of the church.
- **Fear Is Not From God** Many who feel called to ministry hesitate due to fear—fear of rejection, fear of judgment, or fear of stepping out in faith. But God gives power, not fear.
- **Obedience Is the Key to Answering the Call** No matter what opposition arises, our responsibility is to obey God's voice above human traditions.
- **Walking in Freedom Requires Boldness** When God calls, He also provides the strength to walk in His calling. Answering the call requires courage and faith.

Journaling Questions

Journaling provides an opportunity to process what it means to walk in the freedom Christ offers. Have you ever hesitated in responding to God's call because of cultural or church-imposed limitations? Have you allowed fear to keep you from stepping forward?

Through reflection, we can surrender these fears and fully embrace the purpose God has placed in our hearts. Ask the Holy Spirit to reveal areas where you may still be bound by human traditions rather than God's truth.

Understanding Freedom

What does it mean for you personally that Christ has set you free?

_____
_____
_____

Overcoming Fear

Are there fears or doubts that have held you back from fully answering God's call? How can you surrender them?

_____
_____
_____

Recognizing the Holy Spirit's Work

What spiritual gifts has God placed in you that affirm His calling?

_____
_____
_____
_____
_____
_____

Stepping Out in Faith

What specific steps can you take to begin walking in obedience to God's calling on your life?

_____
_____
_____
_____
_____
_____

Encouraging Others

How can you help others step into their own freedom and calling?

_____
_____
_____
_____
_____
_____

Actionable Steps

Cultivate Confidence in Your Calling
Study Scriptures that affirm God's calling on your life and remind yourself of His promises.

Equip Yourself With Biblical Truth
Surround yourself with teachings and mentors who affirm the full scope of God's calling for men and women alike.

Engage in Bold Obedience
Take the first step in faith, whether it's speaking, teaching, leading, or serving. Trust that God has gone before you.

Personal Reflection

Freedom in Christ is more than just a theological concept—it is the reality we are called to walk in. If God has placed a calling on your life, nothing and no one has the authority to revoke it. Have you fully embraced that truth?

Stepping into ministry requires faith, but it also requires the boldness to reject limitations that God never placed on you. If Christ has set you free, then the only question that remains is: Will you walk in that freedom?

If God's Spirit is within you, what is stopping you from stepping forward? Will you trust Him enough to fully answer His call?

_____
_____
_____
_____
_____
_____
_____
_____
_____
_____

Closing Prayer: *Lord, I thank You for the freedom You have given me through Christ. I refuse to be bound by fear, tradition, or human restrictions. I choose to answer Your call with faith and obedience. Equip me, empower me, and let my life be a reflection of the freedom You have given. In Jesus' name, Amen.*

About the Author

Rhonda Garver began her ministry as a missionary in Asia, where she served until the Lord joined her with her husband, Mark Garver. Together, the couple co-pastors Cornerstone Word of Life Church in Madison, Alabama, and leads its Bible Institute and School of Ministry. Known for her strong teaching gift, Rhonda frequently ministers nationally and internationally and hosts Women in Ministry Convocations around the world.

Harrison House is a Spirit-filled, Word of Faith Christian publisher dedicated to spreading the message of faith, hope, and love through our wide range of inspiring publications. Committed to the messages that highlight the power of the Word and Spirit, we provide books, devotionals, and study guides that empower believers to live victorious, faith-filled lives.

Our resources are designed to help readers grow spiritually, strengthen their faith, and experience the transformative power of God's Word. Harrison House is passionate about equipping Christians with the tools they need to fulfill their divine purpose and impact the world for Christ.

www.ingramcontent.com/pod-product-compliance
Lightning Source LLC
Chambersburg PA
CBHW080839230426
43665CB00021B/2889